First published in Great Britain 2024 by Farshore
An imprint of HarperCollins*Publishers*
1 London Bridge Street, London SE1 9GF
www.farshore.co.uk

HarperCollins*Publishers*
Macken House, 39/40 Mayor Street Upper, Dublin 1, D01 C9W8, Ireland

Written by Claire Philip
Images used under license from Shutterstock.com

© The Trustees of the Natural History Museum, London 2024

ISBN 978 0 00 861662 5
Printed and bound in Romania
001

Parental guidance is advised for all craft and colouring activities.
Always ask an adult to help when using glue, paint and scissors.
Wear protective clothing and cover surfaces to avoid staining.
Adult supervision is always necessary when a child is cooking or
using sharp implements.

A CIP catalogue record for this title is available from the British Library.

Stay safe online. Farshore is not responsible for content hosted
by third parties.

MIX
Paper | Supporting
responsible forestry
FSC
www.fsc.org
FSC™ C007454

This book contains FSC™ certified paper and other controlled
sources to ensure responsible forest management.

For more information visit: www.harpercollins.co.uk/green

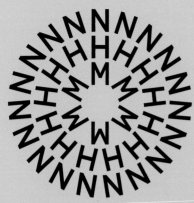

Natural
History
Museum

# DINOSAURS
## ANNUAL 2025

# CONTENTS

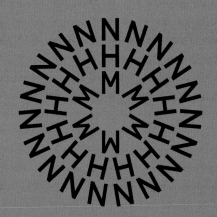

# Natural History Museum

## This book belongs to

......................................................................

......................................................................

Write your name here

Turn the page to turn back time.
Get ready to meet the dinosaurs!

# EXPLORING THE PAST

Our home planet formed around 4.54 billion years ago.
Written out, that's 4,540,000,000 years old! How old are you?

## Early Life

We don't know exactly how life on Earth began, but scientists have two main ideas. One is that tiny living things called microbes arrived on giant space rocks that collided with Earth. The second is that microbes formed in the early oceans, perhaps among the hydrothermal waters on the sea floor.

## Life on Earth Timeline

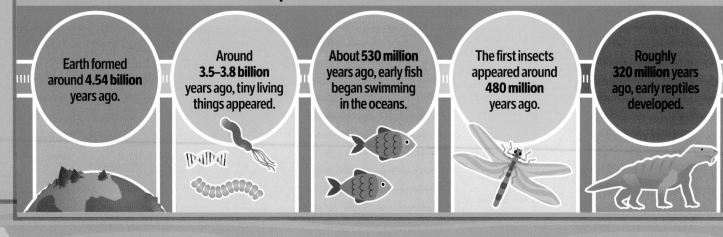

Earth formed around **4.54 billion** years ago.

Around **3.5–3.8 billion** years ago, tiny living things appeared.

About **530 million** years ago, early fish began swimming in the oceans.

The first insects appeared around **480 million** years ago.

Roughly **320 million** years ago, early reptiles developed.

# First Fossils

Some of the earliest fossils are thought to be between 3.5 and 3.8 billion years old. Called stromatolites, these strange rocky structures were built by lots of tiny living things. Life may have existed before 3.8 billion years ago but we don't have the evidence to prove it. Yet!

Stromatolite fossils in Western Australia →

## Dinosaur Timeline

The age of the dinosaurs is divided up into three periods of history.

| The Triassic: 252–201 million years ago the first dinosaurs developed from reptiles | The Jurassic: 201–145 million years ago huge plant-eating dinosaurs appeared | The Cretaceous: 145–66 million years ago many more dinosaurs evolved |
| --- | --- | --- |

**66 million years ago:** a huge extinction event caused the dinosaurs to die out!

About **250 million** years ago, dinosaurs began to roam the planet.

**160 million** years ago, bird-like dinosaurs evolved.

Flowers evolved **130 million** years ago.

**66 million** years ago, the dinosaurs became extinct. Some animals, including mammals, survived.

Between **200,000** and **300,000** years ago, humans that looked similar to us emerged!

# BARYONYX

## A deadly, clawed hunter!

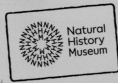 Natural History Museum

## Fish for Tea!

Its body features – and fossil evidence – show that Baryonyx ate a fish-filled diet. It had a long, thin snout with sharp teeth that were perfect for grabbing slippery fish. It also had a 30-centimetre-long claw on each thumb to pierce prey.

## Cretaceous Dino

Baryonyx was a meat-eating theropod dinosaur that lived in the Early Cretaceous period. No one knows why, but it didn't make it to the end of the age of the dinosaurs. It died out around 125 million years ago, long before the mass extinction event that ended the reign of the dinosaurs.

Narrow snout

Crocodile-like teeth

Long neck

Sharp thumb claws

## DINO FACTS

Name: *Baryonyx*

Meaning: *"Heavy Claw"*

Size comparison:

Food: *Fish and other aquatic prey*

Danger rating: *7/10*

Where: *Near shallow water – by lakes and on riverbanks*

## On Two Legs

Baryonyx grew to 9–10 metres in length and weighed roughly 2,000 kilograms – that's the same as a hippopotamus! It belongs to the Spinosauridae dinosaur family, which includes the mighty Spinosaurus and the Suchomimus!

**Spinosaurus**  **Suchomimus**

Long tail

## COLOURING TIME!

Use your favourite pencils to colour in this Baryonyx looking for its dinner.

MINI Activity

BARYONYX

## Bird Family

Theropod dinosaurs are the ancestors of modern-day birds! They were bipedal, meaning they walked on two legs. These dinosaurs ranged in size from less than one metre long (Microraptor) to up to 14 metres in length (Spinosaurus). Famous T. rex was also a theropod.

## Fossil Findings

The very first Baryonyx fossil, a fossilised claw, was discovered around 40 years ago in England! It was the first piece of evidence for a dinosaur that lived partly on land and partly in water. More fossils have been found in Spain and Portugal.

# Colour by Number

Use the colour keys to reveal two prehistoric pictures.

1 blue     2 green     3 orange     4 yellow

1 purple    2 light purple    3 dark purple    4 brown    5 red

6 blue    7 green    8 white    9 pink

13

# CARNOTAURUS

A fearsome, horned and scaly predator!

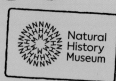
Natural History Museum

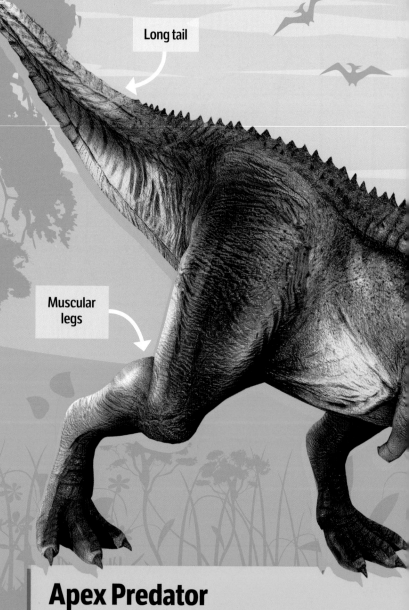

Long tail

Muscular legs

## Tough Skin

This dinosaur had particularly tough skin made up of closely packed scales that looked a bit like a mosaic and would have acted like armour, protecting the Carnotaurus if it was bitten during a tussle with another dinosaur.

## DINO FACTS

Name: *Carnotaurus*

Meaning: *"Meat-eating Bull"*

Size comparison:

Food: *Meat*

Danger rating: *8/10*

Where: *Plains and deserts*

## Apex Predator

A predator is an animal that hunts other animals. Carnotaurus hunted smaller dinosaurs as well as prehistoric mammals and reptiles. Apex means it was at the top of its food chain and wasn't hunted by any other creatures. Can you think of any modern-day apex predators?

## Big Horns

Carnotaurus had a deep skull, muscular neck and two impressive horns above its eyes. It is thought the horns were used for attack or defence, but it is also possible that they helped impress other dinosaurs when it was time to mate.

## One Skeleton

Everything we know about this theropod comes from one single skeleton! It was found in 1984 in South America and took a long time to be removed from the surrounding rock. The skeleton was almost intact and had skin impressions, which is quite rare.

## Fast Sprinter

Carnotaurus was a powerful runner with strong legs. The structure of its skull suggests it also had a great sense of smell, but experts believe it probably relied on its speed – and bone-crushing bite – to make a kill.

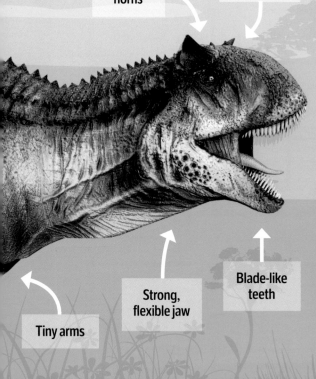

Two large horns

Large brain

Blade-like teeth

Strong, flexible jaw

Tiny arms

## DOT TO DOT!

Join the dots to finish the Carnotaurus, then colour it in!

# Dinosaur Mega Maze

Can you help this Diplodocus collect its eggs and find the way through the maze to its nest?

Answers on page 69.

# Tricky Wordsearch

There are twelve terrifying creatures hidden in the grid below.
Can you find them and spot the odd one out?

Clue:
Read this book
to find the odd
one out.

| O | I | G | H | H | I | U | D | S | Q | J | J | E | K | U | N | N | X | P | W |
| D | I | S | I | D | Q | J | H | E | S | X | E | X | C | U | O | E | Q | W | D |
| V | A | U | F | S | M | O | S | A | S | A | U | R | U | S | R | P | A | C | I |
| H | A | R | U | E | S | I | B | W | E | Q | K | Y | Q | S | Y | Z | S | J | Q |
| K | S | U | V | B | N | O | W | L | F | F | B | B | U | A | A | M | N | J | B |
| N | Z | A | X | U | D | J | G | D | D | F | U | R | E | N | B | T | E | A | L |
| Z | S | S | J | K | S | I | N | O | S | A | U | R | O | P | T | E | R | Y | X |
| O | U | O | O | B | B | U | S | M | Y | A | G | F | H | F | L | Y | X | W | J |
| R | M | T | A | I | H | E | R | J | S | Z | O | A | K | V | O | H | Y | S | M |
| D | I | A | B | X | J | F | V | O | J | K | P | Z | K | N | K | T | P | N | D |
| E | M | P | P | T | R | F | N | S | T | A | V | F | Y | J | Q | R | W | J | Y |
| X | I | A | V | L | W | N | W | G | C | P | Z | X | A | J | D | I | Z | R | Y |
| L | L | M | H | M | A | A | H | D | L | H | A | H | R | A | Z | C | A | D | S |
| H | L | C | D | R | B | K | S | E | K | R | R | R | E | D | L | E | F | V | F |
| Z | A | J | Y | G | S | U | R | U | A | S | O | N | I | Z | I | R | E | H | T |
| Y | G | T | B | P | N | C | S | G | T | D | A | D | D | V | T | A | R | Z | B |
| F | B | B | N | H | D | I | M | E | T | R | O | D | O | N | O | T | B | L | F |
| D | I | P | L | O | D | O | C | U | S | Y | S | Z | W | G | F | O | Y | I | D |
| T | R | W | U | C | S | U | R | U | A | T | O | N | R | A | C | P | M | N | X |
| S | Y | K | M | E | M | J | C | W | U | Z | C | A | U | R | Z | S | G | X | O |

- [ ] **BARYONYX**
- [ ] **CARNOTAURUS**
- [ ] **GALLIMIMUS**
- [ ] **OVIRAPTOR**
- [ ] **APATOSAURUS**
- [ ] **DIPLODOCUS**
- [ ] **SINOSAUROPTERYX**
- [ ] **THERIZINOSAURUS**
- [ ] **DIMETRODON**
- [ ] **TRICERATOPS**
- [ ] **MOSASAURUS**
- [ ] **TYRANNOSAURUS REX**

*Answers on page 69.*

# WHAT IS EVOLUTION?

Ever wondered why some dinosaurs were tall with long necks when others had wings, or big spikes?

## Who was Darwin?

The scientist Charles Darwin is often called the 'father of evolution'. Whilst he didn't focus his studies on dinosaur fossils, his most important theory - of how animals adapt to their environments to survive - helped future paleontologists understand how dinosaurs lived and changed over time.

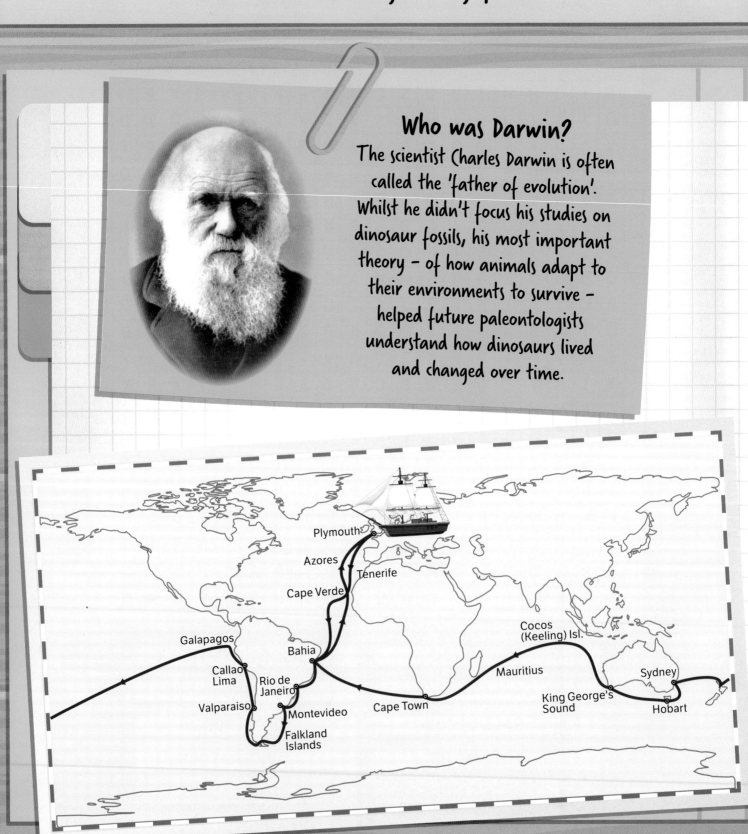

Plymouth
Azores
Tenerife
Cape Verde
Galapagos
Bahia
Callao
Lima
Rio de
Janeiro
Valparaiso
Montevideo
Cape Town
Falkland
Islands
Cocos
(Keeling) Isl.
Mauritius
Sydney
King George's
Sound
Hobart

## Super Collector

In 1831, when he was 22 years old, Darwin spent five years sailing the world on a British Navy ship called HMS Beagle. He collected, examined and recorded the animal and plant species he found on his journey. Later, he wrote a very famous book, called 'On the Origin of Species' about his findings and his theory of evolution.

## Natural Selection

Darwin's observations helped him describe natural selection — the way in which a species changes in response to its environment. Successful species develop the traits they need to survive and pass them on to their offspring. Unsuccessful species die out.

## Dinosaur Diversity

Experts believe the dinosaurs lived so long because they managed to keep up as Earth's environment changed. There was a huge peak in dinosaur diversity during the Cretaceous period as Earth's continents (land masses) split further apart. This sparked lots of animal adaptations.

## Fantastic Finches

Darwin famously visited the Galápagos Islands off the west coast of South America. He realised later that the finches there were all slightly different to the ones he saw on the mainland. He concluded that they each had physical traits that helped them find food in their unique habitats.

# GALLIMIMUS

## A fast and agile bird-like dinosaur!

Natural History Museum

## Hide and Seek

Some theories suggest that predators of the Gallimimus could have had colour vision, leading scientists to believe that Gallimimus could have developed camouflaged skin or feathers to protect itself.

## Long but Light!

Gallimimus lived during the Late Cretaceous period and is the largest known member of the feathered ornithomimid dinosaur group. Fossils found in the Gobi Desert in Mongolia show that it had a slender, lightweight body and grew to approximately 6 metres in length.

← Long legs

## DINO FACTS

Name: *Gallimimus*

Meaning: *"Chicken Mimic"*

Size comparison:

Food: *Most likely an omnivore (both plants and animals)*

Danger rating: *4/10*

Where: *Near water, plains, woodlands*

## Side Eyes

This bird-like dinosaur had eyes on the side of its head, which would have helped it keep an eye out for large predators such as the Tarbosaurus, the second largest member of the Tyrannosaurus dinosaur family.

Eyes on side of its head

Small head

Narrow beak

Long neck

Hollow bones

## Beaked Mouth

Gallimimus had a beak and no teeth! It is difficult to know exactly what this dinosaur dined on but it may have eaten small animals, eggs and plants. Some experts believe it may have even been a filter-feeding animal, sucking up water and filtering out tiny little creatures called zooplankton to eat. Slurp!

## Like a Bird

The name Gallimimus means 'chicken mimic' but it, like other members of its family, was much more like an ostrich and probably ran like one as well. Experts think it could have potentially reached a seriously speedy 34 miles per hour.

# FIND THE ODD ONE OUT

MINI Activity

Draw lines to match the dinosaur pairs, and circle the dinosaur without a match.

Answers on page 69.

# Prehistoric Paper Folding

Learn the ancient art of paper folding! Carefully follow the instructions below to create these simple origami dinosaurs.

**1** Place your square of paper as shown here and using these lines as a guide, carefully fold each point into the centre of the paper. Unfold.

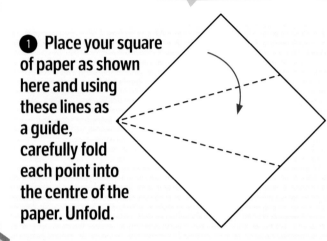

**2** Refold the top point towards the centre, then fold it in half back on itself. Make sure that point overlaps the edge of the model at the top.

**3** Repeat the process for the bottom corner, folding upwards.

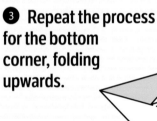

**4** Now fold this corner in half back on itself, making sure the point overlaps the edge of the model at the bottom.

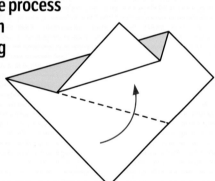

**5** Now turn the whole piece of paper over, you should have a model of a Plesiosaur with two fins poking out beneath it.

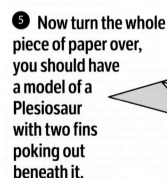

**6** To decorate your model you will need to add some scales and eyes – you can either draw them or cut small circles from paper and stick them on.

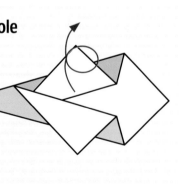

## Origami Plesiosaur

For each origami model you will need:
- a square piece of plain paper measuring 21cm x 21cm
- colouring pencils to decorate.

**1** Take your piece of square paper and carefully fold it in half diagonally, making a firm crease, then unfold your square.

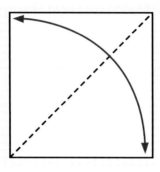

**2** Now fold the paper in half diagonally, the opposite way to step 1, making another firm crease. Keep it folded this time.

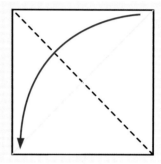

**3** Fold back the top layer of paper from the bottom left hand corner, and fold in half so the point ends just before the long edge.

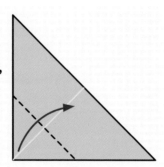

**4** Fold the triangle in half, away from yourself. Taking the top left corner (a) behind to the right bottom corner (b).

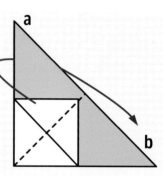

**5** Fold the bottom left hand corner up, making sure the fold sits above the main triangle as this will be the Triceratops' horn.

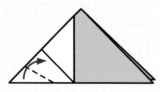

**6** Make sure all your creases are firm and keeping their shape. Now turn the model over.

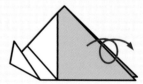

**7** Take the top layer of paper from the left hand corner and make a crease, so that the fold sits at a right angle to the body to support it.

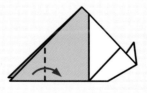

**8** Now your Triceratops needs colouring in! Add eyes, scales and extra horns to your awesome origami model.

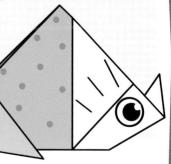

# Origami Triceratops

Difficulty Rating: **TRICKY**

# OVIRAPTOR

A small, beaked theropod.

Natural History Museum

## Broody Parents

Clear fossil evidence shows an Oviraptor on top of a nest. This suggests that, like most modern-day birds, it sat on its eggs to keep them warm until they hatched. If so, it may have taken care of its hatchlings for a short while, too.

## The Wrong Name

Oviraptor lived in the Late Cretaceous period and was discovered in Mongolia. It was first thought Oviraptor stole eggs from other dinosaurs, so it was given a name that means egg thief, but no one knows for sure.

## Parrot-like Beak

Oviraptor had a parrot-like beak, which has led experts to believe it probably ate crunchy eggs and shellfish. Its jaws would have been perfect for cracking into hard shells or even prehistoric crustaceans. Yum!

Beak-like mouth

No teeth

## DINO FACTS

Name: *Oviraptor*

Meaning: *"Egg Thief"*

Size comparison:

Food: *Eggs, shellfish and plants*

Danger rating: *2/10*

Where: *Deserts and forested areas*

Curved claws

Can you piece the path back together and help the dinosaur reach the egg?

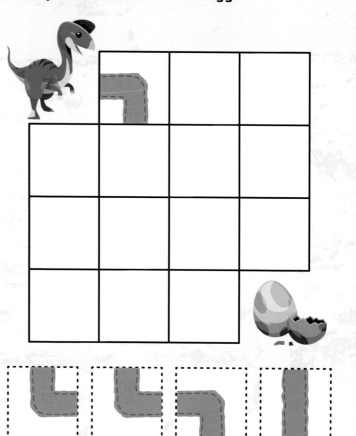

Answers on page 69.

## Small Size

This dinosaur grew to around 2 metres long and weighed about 40 kilograms – that's the size of a tall adult human and the weight of an emperor penguin!

Feathers

## Feathered Body

While not definitely proven, scientists are pretty certain this dinosaur was fully covered in feathers. The tail feathers may have functioned as a way to attract mates. Perhaps they waved them like a peacock!

**Glossary box:**

A **crustacean** is an animal with a hard outer shell instead of an internal skeleton. They often have many pairs of legs and live in the water.

# How to Draw a Dinosaur

**Follow the steps below to draw your very own dinosaur friend.**

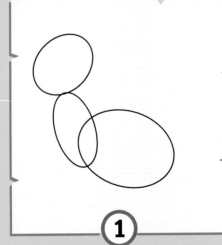

**(1)** Using a pencil to sketch the lines lightly, start by drawing three overlapping ovals for the head, neck and body.

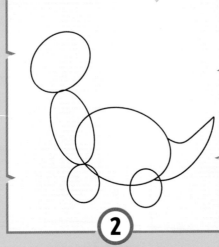

**(2)** Add a tail and two circles for legs.

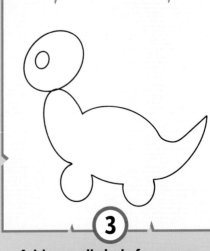

**(3)** Add a small circle for an eye. Now take some time to carefully rub out any overlapping lines you don't need.

**(4)** Draw lines to connect the neck to the head, rubbing out any lines you don't need. Now add a smile.

**(5)** Lastly, add some wiggly lines along the head and back, small circles on the body for scales and lines on the feet.

**(6)** Now colour in your dino using this picture as a guide. Leave some white on the eyes, head and tail for highlights.

Can you add in lots of extra details, such as rocks, leaves, some clouds and a volcano?

# THE PREHISTORIC WORLD

Dinosaurs were alive during the Mesozoic Era, 252–66 million years ago. During that time, the natural world around them changed a lot.

## Massive Shifts

During the Triassic period — the first period of the Mesozoic era — all of the land on Earth was joined together in a supercontinent called Pangaea. By the end of the Cretaceous period — the last period of the Mesozoic era — Earth's land masses looked similar to today.

**252 Million Years Ago**

**Present day**

### Triassic 252–201 million years ago

**Landscape:** In the Triassic, Earth had many deserts and there were no icy polar regions

**Types of dinos:** Coelophysis, Eoraptor, Herrerasaurus, Procompsognathus, Plateosaurus

**Other creatures:** Small mammals, turtles, crocodile-like creatures, centipedes, scorpions, flying reptiles

**In the oceans:** Ammonites, molluscs, corals, plesiosaurs, ichthyosaurs

**Landmass:** Pangaea started to split apart into two super-continents named Laurasia and Gondwana.

## The Great Dying

Before the very first dinosaurs emerged, there was a mass extinction event now known as the Great Dying. It is thought to be Earth's largest extinction event, an estimated 95% of all species on Earth were wiped out! Extinction events like this have happened a few times throughout history.

**Glossary box:**

**Extinction** is when a species completely dies out. An **era** is a major length of time divided up into smaller sections known as **periods**.

A **species** is a group of organisms that can reproduce. Cats, dolphins and humans are all species!

## Jurassic 201–145 million years ago

**Landscape:** During the Jurassic, the climate was warmer and more stable. Forests flourished and the first flowering plants, called angiosperms, emerged

**Types of dinos:** Brachiosaurus, Diplodocus, Stegosaurus, Allosaurus, feathered dinosaurs

**Other creatures:** Early mammals, flying reptiles called pterosaurs, flying insects

**In the oceans:** Marine reptiles, plesiosaurs, fish, squid

**Landmass:** Laurasia started to split apart to form the Eurasian and North American continents, whilst a rift in Gondwana started to form what is now South America, Africa and Australia.

## Cretaceous 145–66 million years ago

**Landscape:** The climate of the Cretaceous was warm and humid, which led to an amazing abundance of life

**Types of dinos:** Triceratops, hadrosaurs, Tyrannosaurus Rex, bird-like dinosaurs

**Other creatures:** Early mammals, bees, snakes, pterosaurs

**In the oceans:** Mosasaurs, plesiosaurs, pliosaurs, sharks, fish, marine reptiles

**Landmass:** Distinct continents begin to take shape and move into their current positions and the oceans between them start to form.

# APATOSAURUS

A giant, long-necked plant-eater.

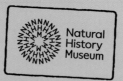

Natural History Museum

Small head

## The Biggest of All?

This massive sauropod dinosaur lived during the Late Jurassic period alongside other giant herbivores such as Diplodocus. At around 21 metres long, it may have been one of the largest dinosaurs of all time.

## New Name!

Apatosaurus used to be known as Brontosaurus! The fossils of this dinosaur were originally thought to be from separate species, but experts worked out that they were actually the same creature. The name Apatosaurus was kept as it had come first. Sorry Brontosaurus!

## Mega Body

Fossils of Apatosaurus found in North America show that it had a small head for its body size, a whip-like tail and an extremely large body. Estimates on its weight vary but it probably weighed around 24,000 kg, the equivalent of four elephants!

## DINO FACTS

Name: *Apatosaurus*
(*previously known as Brontosaurus*)

Meaning: *"Deceptive Lizard"*

Size comparison:

Food: *Plants*

Danger rating: *3/10*

Where: *Floodplains, woodlands*

## Leafy Dinners

Like large grazing animals alive today, Apatosaurus would have had to eat a lot of food to make sure it had enough energy to stay alive. It probably spent most of its days grazing on available plants. Munch!

## Big Eggs

Sauropod dinosaurs hatched from huge eggs! Fossilised Apatosaurus eggs have been found measuring around 30 centimetres across! It is thought that these dinosaurs simply laid eggs as they were walking along, rather than making bird-like nests. Plop!

Chicken egg        Apatosaurus egg

# FINDING FOOD

MINI Activity

Follow the wiggly lines to help the dinosaur find the leafy tree for its dinner!

Answers on page 69.

Huge body

**Glossary box:**

**Sauropods** had very long necks and tails. They ate plants and walked on four legs.

**Herbivores** are plant-eating animals.

Long tail

Four pillar-like legs

# Meteoric Maths!

Can you solve these tricky sums and use the colour/number key to complete the prehistoric picture?

= 3     = 4     = 5     = 6

a)     − − =

b)     + − =

c)     − + =

d)     + + =

e)     − + =

**Colour by number key**

1   2   3   4   5   6   7   8

# DIPLODOCUS

Natural History Museum

A long-necked sauropod with a whip-like tail!

## Giant Whip

It is thought that Diplodocus could make a very loud sound by whipping its flexible tail. This may have been a communication tool or perhaps a way to defend itself. It is believed that the meat-eating theropod Allosaurus may have hunted younger, smaller Diplodocus – the adults were probably too large for them to take down.

## DINO FACTS

Name: *Diplodocus*

Meaning: *"Double Beam"*

Size comparison:

Food: *Plants*

Danger rating: *2/10*

Where: *Floodplains, woodlands*

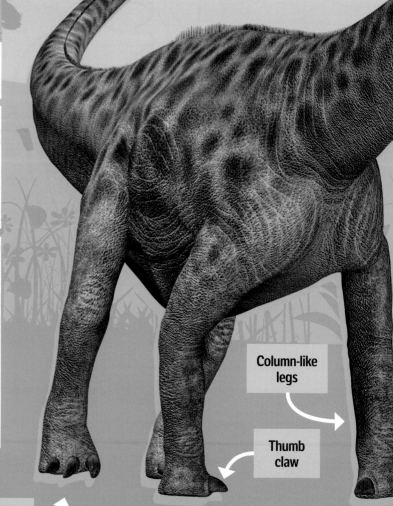

Super long tail for balance.

Column-like legs

Thumb claw

Back legs longer than front legs

**Glossary box:**

**Vertebrae** are the small bones that make up an animal's backbone.

Small head

Rows of peg-like teeth

Long neck to reach high plants.

## Rows of Teeth

Did you know Diplodocus had rows of teeth at the front of its mouth? It's true! This toothy dinosaur would regularly shed its long, thin teeth after stripping masses of tough vegetation. The teeth that fell out were then replaced by the next row!

## Up High

Diplodocus was a giant sauropod dinosaur that lived during the Late Jurassic period. It had an incredibly long neck made up of 15 vertebrae – that's almost half the number a human has in their whole back bone! Scientists aren't certain, but this adaptation could have meant it ate leaves on high-growing trees.

## Tummy Stones

Some animals swallow stones to help them break down food! Diplodocus and other sauropod dinosaur fossils have been found with these rocks, called gastroliths, perfectly preserved in their bellies.

MINI Activity

## SHADOW MATCH!

Only one of these shadows matches this dinosaur picture, can you spot which one?

a

b

c

d

Answers on page 69.

# Necks and Tails Game

Grab a friend and take it in turns to roll the dice and move your counter around the board.

**How to Play:**
The first person to reach the finish wins! Watch out for the dinosaur necks that will allow you to move forward and the dinosaur tails that move you backwards on the board.

*You will need: a counter or a coin per player and a dice.*

23  22  21

24

25

26

27

28  29  30

41

42

43

44

START

1  2  3

# EXTREME EXTINCTION

At the end of the Cretaceous period there was a catastrophic natural event that ended the dinosaurs' reign.

## The End For Many

A giant asteroid crashed into Earth from space. The impact caused deadly wildfires to rage and huge storms to form. Dust and debris in the air blocked out sunlight, causing Earth's temperatures to drop. All of these changes destroyed food chains, making the planet unliveable for many species.

## Mega Crater

Most scientists agree that the dinosaurs died out due to the effects of an enormous asteroid impact. The giant space rock crashed into the Earth's surface leaving a crater 150 kilometres wide! The crater in Mexico is still visible today (although a lot of it is underwater). It's called the Chicxulub crater.

A smaller impact site in Arizona, USA shows what an asteroid crater looks like.

## Some Survivors

Luckily for us, not all of life on Earth was destroyed! Around one quarter of species survived. The mammal animal group had been previously overshadowed by dinosaurs, but now it had the chance to adapt to a new Earth. The ancestors of modern birds (called non-avian dinosaurs) also survived!

**Glossary box:**

When one animal eats another animal, and then that animal is eaten by another animal, a **food chain** is formed.

## Extinction Timeline

This table shows that mass extinctions (when lots of living species die at the same time) have happened multiple times throughout history. While we have good evidence to explain some of the events, not all of them are fully understood.

| Event name | What happened? | Estimated Species Extinction rate |
|---|---|---|
| Ordovician-Silurian | **443 million years ago** sea levels dropped dramatically and temperatures quickly rose. | **85%** |
| Devonian | **374 million years ago** nearly three quarters of life on Earth became extinct. We don't know why for sure, but changes in the Earth's environment and the gases in the atmosphere may have been part of it. | **75%** |
| Permian-Triassic (The Great Dying) | **250 million years ago** a large asteroid impact or enormous volcano eruption wiped out almost all species. | **95%** |
| Triassic | **200 million years ago** temperatures rose and the oceans became more acidic, harming life. | **80%** |
| Cretaceous | **66 million years ago** an asteroid impact caused devastating living conditions for most creatures including all dinosaurs. | **78%** |

# SINOSAUROPTERYX

**A tiny feathered theropod!**

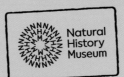

Natural History Museum

## Found in China

Sinosauropteryx was a theropod dinosaur from the Early Cretaceous period. It was the first ever dinosaur to be discovered with feather-like structures! At only one metre in length and weighing only 0.5 kilograms, it was a tiny dinosaur!

## Colourful Creature

It is extremely rare for fossils to give any evidence of colouring; yet fossil analysis of Sinosauropteryx suggests its feathers were probably a red-orange colour. It may have also had a striped tail!

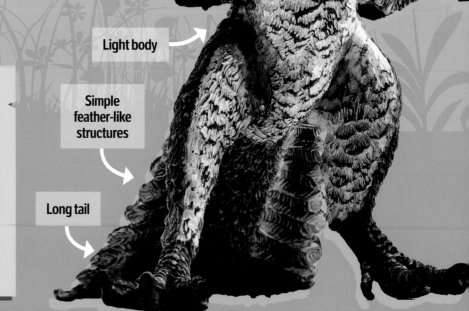

Short arms

Light body

Simple feather-like structures

Long tail

## Full Stomach

We know that Sinosauropteryx was a meat-eater thanks to fossil evidence – the remains of small mammals were found preserved in one fossilised stomach, while another contained the remains of a lizard!

# DINO FACTS

Name: *Sinosauropteryx*

Meaning: *"Chinese Lizard Wing"*

Size comparison:

Food: *Meat, likely insects and small vertebrates*

Danger rating: *2/10*

Where: *Forested areas, near water*

## Flightless Feathers

Dinosaurs such as Sinosauropteryx could have evolved early feathers for a number of reasons beyond flight. One of the most convincing theories is that they may have kept the animals warm in cold conditions. This is called insulation.

Three fingers

## HOW MANY WORDS?

**MINI Activity**

My name is Sinosauropteryx. How many words can you make from the letters in my name?

# SINOSAUROPTERYX

### Glossary box:

Some animals have **camouflage** – body features that allow them to blend into their environment.

Answers on page 69.

# Cretaceous Cookies

Bake and decorate these delicious dinosaur cookies whenever you need a tasty treat.

## You will need:

- Baking trays lined with baking paper
- Dinosaur shaped cookie cutters or a knife
- Mixing bowl
- Wooden spoon
- Rolling pin

## Ingredients:

### For the Cookies

- 90 grams unsalted butter, very soft
- 100 grams caster sugar
- 1 large egg, beaten
- ½ teaspoon vanilla extract
- 200 grams plain flour
- ½ teaspoon baking powder
- ½ teaspoon salt

### For the Icing

- 150 grams icing sugar
- Few drops of water
- Food colouring

Ask an adult to help !

42

## Instructions:

**1** Preheat the oven to 180°C/160°C fan, gas mark 4.

**2** Cream together the butter and sugar until pale.

**3** Add the egg and the vanilla extract, beating until smooth.

**4** Add the rest of the ingredients and mix until you have a firm dough.

**5** Rest the dough in the fridge for half an hour.

**6** Roll out the dough on a floured surface to the thickness of about ½ cm.

**7** Cut out dinosaur shapes and place on the lined baking trays. Ask an adult to put them in the oven for you.

**8** Bake in the oven for 10 minutes, or until golden brown.

**9** Leave to cool. Make the icing by gradually adding a few drops of water and food colouring at a time and mixing well until you have a thick spreadable icing (if it gets too runny add some more icing sugar).

**10** Decorate your dinos! You could create this fossil effect with white icing or get creative with colourful icing and sprinkles.

# THERIZINOSAURUS

## A plant-eating dinosaur with curved claws!

 Natural History Museum

## DINO FACTS

Name: *Therizinosaurus*

Meaning: *"Scythe Lizard"*

Size comparison:

Food: *Plants*

Danger rating: *2/10*

Where: *Most likely woodland*

Small head

Long neck

Long, curved claws

Bulky body

Wide hips

Stood upright on two legs

## Scythe Claws

Therizinosaurus was an extremely unusual theropod dinosaur that lived during the Late Cretaceous period. It is best known for its long, scythe-shaped claws, which at one metre long are the longest claws of any animal ever found!

## Desert Fossils

The first Therizinosaurus fossils, including these eggs, were found in the Gobi Desert in Mongolia in 1948. At first, scientists thought they belonged to a turtle-like creature but later, when a forearm bone was discovered, they realised that it was a dinosaur!

## Big and Feathery?

Reconstructions of Therizinosaurus based on fossil findings estimate that it weighed an impressive 5–6 tonnes and grew to around 10 metres in length. A close relative of Therizinosaurus had feathers, so it may well have done so, too.

## Plant-Eater

Most theropod dinosaurs were meat-eaters, but some scientists think that Therizinosaurus used its claws to grab plants to eat – a bit like an enormous sloth! Another theory is that they were used in self-defence or as a signal to other dinosaurs that they were fully grown.

## WHICH WAY?

MINI Activity

Find the right wiggly line that leads Therizinosaurus to the eggs!

1

2

3

# Colour in Diplodocus

Colour in this picture of a Diplodocus by the muddy bank of a river.
Can you draw in some dinosaur footprints too?

# Missing Piece Puzzle

Find the pieces of the puzzle that fell out of the picture.

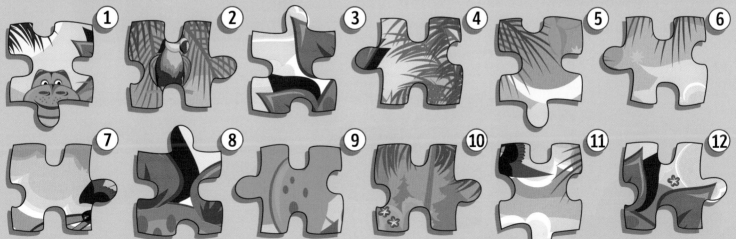

Once you have found which pieces are missing, can you try and draw them in the correct spaces to complete the picture?

# RESEARCH SCIENTISTS

Research scientists study dinosaur remains to learn about how they lived. They look at fossils, footprints, nests, eggs and even poo!

### Back in the Lab

The fossils are then taken back to a laboratory to be examined. Sometimes the scientists make models of their findings. They do this by taking x-rays from many different angles. A computer takes all of these images and combines them into one 3D image.

### Fossil Digs

Field expeditions are special trips to places that contain dinosaur fossils or other evidence of their activity. They are often in remote places that are hard to reach! Research scientists set up camp, then carefully dig up the fossils over a number of weeks, months or even years!

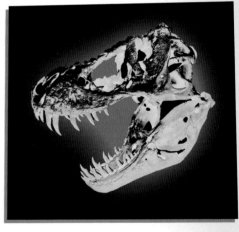

x-ray

Coprolite (fossilised dinosaur poo)

**Glossary box:**

**Climate change** is the term used to describe the changes in Earth's temperature and weather systems.

## Did You Know?

Research scientists are super important because their work helps us learn about evolution and climate change — as well as the history of life on Earth. Sometimes they make amazing new discoveries and other times they prove or disprove important theories. Would you like to be a research scientist?

## How Old?

Scientists drill into dinosaur fossils to find out how old they are. They take samples from inside the bone and examine them closely. This can be useful when lots of scattered bones are found in one place. If the bones are all the same age they may be from the same dinosaur.

A fossil tooth from a theropod dinosaur

# DIMETRODON

Natural History Museum

A prehistoric creature that predated the dinosaurs.

Large back sail

## Mammal Ancestor

Even though it looks remarkably like a dinosaur, Dimetrodon was actually a synapsid – an early ancestor of mammals. It lived millions of years before the dinosaurs evolved and was an apex predator of its day.

## Sail Back

Dimetrodon is easily recognised by its large back sail. Spines grew from its vertebrae and were joined by skin. This distinctive body feature may have functioned as a way to attract mates or perhaps to regulate its body temperature. What do you think?

## DINO FACTS

Name: *Dimetrodon*

Meaning: *"Two Measures of Teeth"*

Size comparison:

Food: *Meat*

Danger rating: *3/10*

Where: *Swamps*

Long tail

## What is a Synapsid?

A synapsid is an animal with a backbone belonging to the Synapsida group. These creatures had a single opening behind the eye socket. This opening was important as it enabled powerful jaw muscles that could chew all kinds of food – an evolutionary advantage!

# SEARCH AND FIND

MINI Activity

Scan this dinosaur scene to find **6** dinosaurs hidden in the picture!

Dimetrodon

Yulong

Supersaurus

Pteradon

Lambeosaurus

Stegosaurus

Two types of teeth

Walked on four legs

## Two Teeth

This prehistoric creature is named after its two different sets of teeth! One set was long and sharp and one was serrated, like a knife. Dimetrodon would have had a seriously deadly bite. **Chomp!**

Fossil of a pelycosaur, a mammal-like reptile sometimes called a sail reptile or synapsid amniote, from the Permian or Triassic Period.

# Dinosaur Hunt

Time to test your observation skills. Can you study this picture and find the 10 objects shown on the right?

Answers on page 69.

# TRICERATOPS

Natural History Museum

An enormous plant-eater with sharp horns and a bony frill.

## Late Dinosaur

Triceratops is a ceratopsid dinosaur from the Late Cretaceous period. It lived 68–66 million years ago and died out during the extinction event that killed off almost all of the dinosaurs. Scientists have found lots of their fossils, including some that show multiple Triceratops in one place.

## Large Horns

Triceratops is best known for its three horns, which, depending on the species of Triceratops, could grow from 60 centimetres to one metre in length! They were probably used in defence or in combat. If Triceratops charged, the horns could have delivered a whopping blow. Watch out!

Three sharp forward-facing horns

Bony neck frill

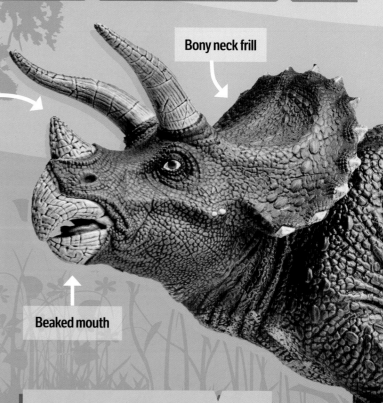

Beaked mouth

## DINO FACTS

Name: *Triceratops*

Meaning: *"Three-Horned Face"*

Size comparison:

Food: *Plants*

Danger rating: *1/10*

Where: *Coasts, floodplains, forested areas*

## Adapted for Plants

Triceratops' mouth was perfectly adapted for its diet of plants. Its sharp-edged beak would have allowed it to slice through vegetation such as cycads, conifers and palms.

# PREHISTORIC PIXEL ART

MINI
Activity

Draw your very own Triceratops in the empty grid by copying the grid on the left!

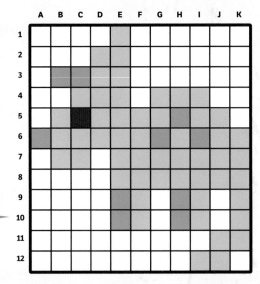

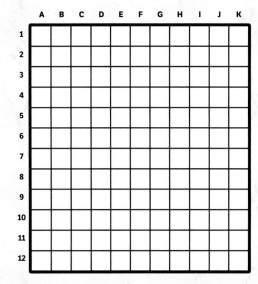

Huge body

## Herd Animal

Fossil evidence suggests that Triceratops may have lived in herds. It may have done this for protection from predators or to find food. It is also possible that they came together to mate. Experts believe it was quite common for plant-eaters to live together in big groups.

Short legs

**Glossary box:**

A **ceratopsid** is a dinosaur from the horned, herbivorous Ceratopsidae group. Styracosaurus and Centrosaurus were also ceratopsids.

# Dino Footprint Tangle

Do you know what a dinosaur's footprints would have looked like?
Follow these footsteps to see where they lead.

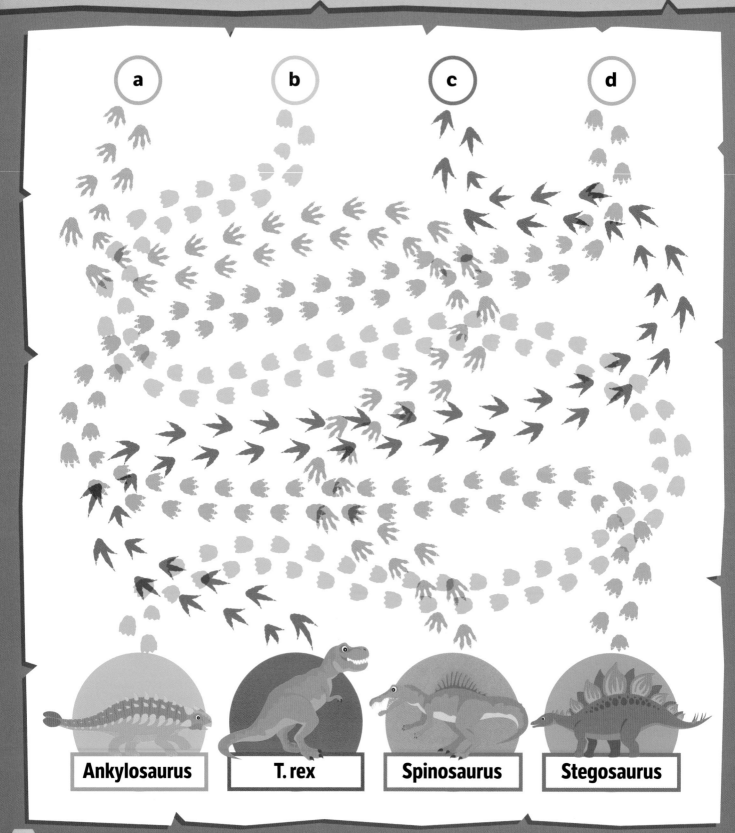

a b c d

**Ankylosaurus** **T. rex** **Spinosaurus** **Stegosaurus**

*Answers on page 69.*

# Which Dino Are You?

Imagine you were a dinosaur! Answer these five questions to find out which dinosaur you would have been.

**Question 1:**

Where would you prefer to live?

- **a** In grassland
- **b** In a forest
- **c** In or near the water

**Question 2:**

What is your preferred mode of transportation?

- **a** Walking on four legs
- **b** Running on two legs
- **c** Swimming

**Question 3:**

How do you like to defend yourself?

- **a** With armour or spikes
- **b** With sharp teeth and powerful jaws
- **c** By staying hidden in the water

**Question 4:**

What is your favourite food?

- **a** Plants and leaves
- **b** Meat
- **c** Fish

**Question 5:**

What's your personality like?

- **a** Peaceful and gentle
- **b** Fierce and dominant
- **c** Curious and agile

## Answers:

**Mostly a :**
**You are a Stegosaurus!**

You're a herbivore that roamed the grasslands during the Jurassic period. You are known for the distinctive plates on your back and your tail spikes.

**Mostly b :**
**You are a T. rex!**

You're a sharp toothed carnivore, roaming the forest, the apex predator of the Late Cretaceous period, and known for your deadly bite.

**Mostly c :**
**You are a Plesiosaurus!**

You're a marine reptile that lived in the ocean during the Mesozoic era, known for your long neck and flipper-like limbs for swimming.

# NEWS AND DISCOVERIES

Each year we learn more about dinosaurs as new fossils are found or research is undertaken. Here are some recently reported exciting finds.

An extremely interesting discovery in China shows a hunt scene between a badger-like mammal and a **Psittacosaurus** dinosaur! A fossil has been discovered that shows the mammal biting into the ribs of the beaked dinosaur. This is important because it shows us that dinosaurs could be wounded by mammals that were smaller than them.

## NEW NAMED SPECIES OF ANKYLOSAUR

A new species of Ankylosaur has been named! Vectipelta barretti was found on the Isle of Wight, UK, and is named after the prominent scientist Paul Barrett. Ankylosaurs were planteating dinosaurs with great defences from predators – they were covered in armoured plates and spikes! **Vectipelta barretti's** spikes were like blades!

A Psittacosaurus fossil.

Titanosaur herd

# 200 EGGS!

Fossilised dinosaur eggs

More than **200** Titanosaur eggs have been found in India! The researchers studied an amazing **92** nests to learn as much as they could about how these enormous dinosaurs reproduced. They think that they may have laid eggs closely together – but then left them behind.

# PROPOSAL!

A new Spinosaur called **Protathlitis cinctorrensis** has been proposed! Fossilised vertebrae and a section of jaw were found in Spain. Recent examination of these findings indicate that Spinosaurs may have evolved in the west of Europe.

# NEW DISCOVERY ALERT!

**A new species of** theropod dinosaur from the early Cretaceous has been found in Mongolia, China. This dinosaur, named **Migmanychion laiyang**, is notable for its unusual finger bones!

**Minimocursor phunoiensis** is the name of a two-metre high dinosaur newly discovered at a fossil site nicknamed Thailand's Jurassic Park. It is remarkably well preserved!

# MOSASAURUS

A deadly, reptilian ocean hunter.

Natural History Museum

## Mighty Reptile!

Mosasaurus wasn't a dinosaur, it was a massive marine reptile that lived towards the end of the age of the dinosaurs – it died out during the same extinction event. It was named after the Meuse River in the Netherlands, close to where early fossils were found.

## Air Breather

Mosasaurus was a fearsome ocean predator with a body perfectly adapted to hunting beneath the waves. It would have come up to the water's surface regularly to breathe air before diving back down to search for prey.

## DINO FACTS

Name: *Mosasaurus*

Meaning: *"Meuse Lizard"*

Size comparison:

Food: *Meat, preyed on fish, ammonites and other marine reptiles*

Danger rating: *7/10*

Where: *Water*

Sharp teeth

Powerful jaws

Flipper-like limbs

## Ocean Babies

Fossil studies suggest that Mosasaurus lived in the open ocean. Rather than laying eggs on land, like turtles, (oviparous), they would have given birth to live young in the water (viviparous).

## Open Wide

This super predator was a skilled swimmer and would have hunted fish, sharks, marine reptiles and smaller mosasaurs. It could open its jaw wide enough to swallow prey in one go and had super sharp, spike-like teeth.

Streamlined body

Smooth scales

MINI Activity

## COPY THE PATH

Copy the lines on picture **a** to make a path on picture **b** for the Mosasaurus to get to the marine reptile!

**a**

**b**

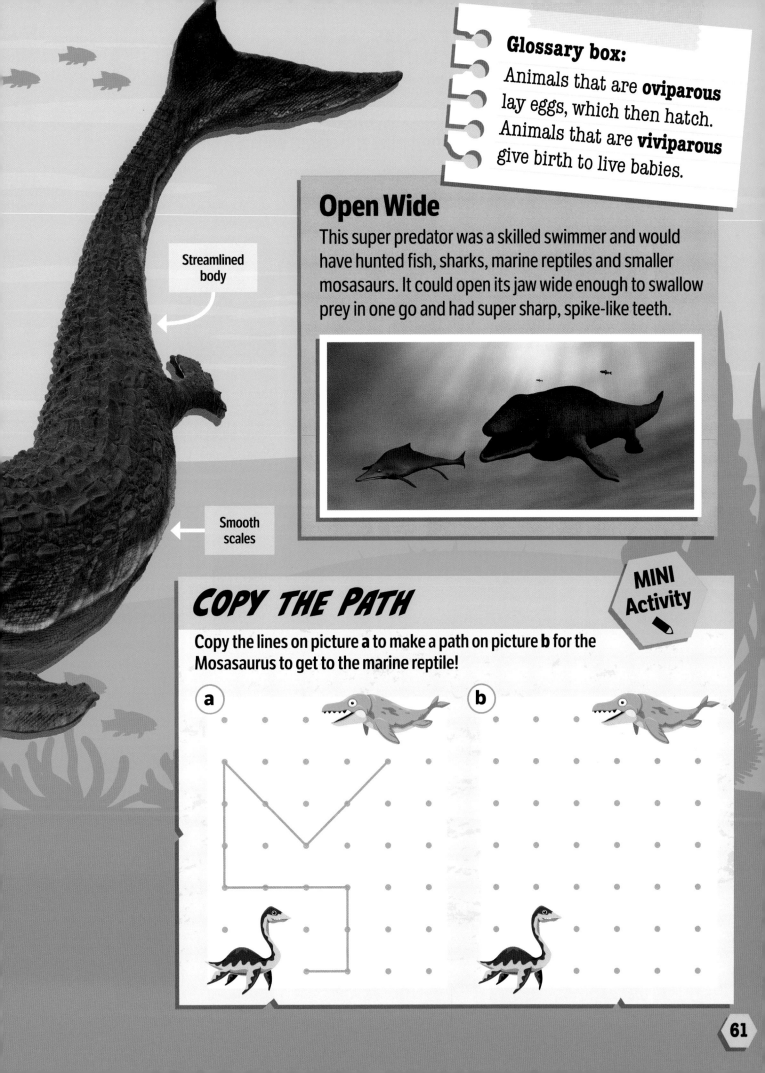

# Super Statistics Game

Enjoy learning about the super statistics for the dinosaurs below, then play the game with a friend.

## Tyrannosaurus rex

*Size:* **9 metres**
*Length:* **12.2 metres**
*Weight:* **8 metric tons**
*Speed:* **40.2 km/h**
*Danger Rating:* **10**

## Triceratops

*Size:* **8 metres**
*Length:* **9.1 metres**
*Weight:* **12 metric tons**
*Speed:* **32.2 km/h**
*Danger Rating:* **7**

## Velociraptor

*Size:* **2 metres**
*Length:* **1.8 metres**
*Weight:* **68 kilograms**
*Speed:* **64.4 km/h**
*Danger Rating:* **9**

## Stegosaurus

*Size:* **7 metres**
*Length:* **9.1 metres**
*Weight:* **5.4 metric tons**
*Speed:* **8 km/h**
*Danger Rating:* **6**

## Brachiosaurus

*Size:* **10 metres**
*Length:* **22.9 metres**
*Weight:* **50 metric tons**
*Speed:* **16 km/h**
*Danger Rating:* **5**

## Allosaurus

*Size:* **9 metres**
*Length:* **12.2 metres**
*Weight:* **8 metric tons**
*Speed:* **40.2 km/h**
*Danger Rating:* **10**

## Ankylosaurus

*Size:* **7 metres**
*Length:* **7.6 metres**
*Weight:* **5.4 metric tons**
*Speed:* **8 km/h**
*Danger Rating:* **7**

## Spinosaurus

*Size:* **9 metres**
*Length:* **15.2 metres**
*Weight:* **12 metric tons**
*Speed:* **32.2 km/h**
*Danger Rating:* **9**

## Diplodocus

*Size:* **9 metres**
*Length:* **27.4 metres**
*Weight:* **15 metric tons**
*Speed:* **24.1 km/h**
*Danger Rating:* **4**

## Pteranodon

*Size:* **4 metres**
*Length:* **6 metres wingspan**
*Weight:* **22.7 kilograms**
*Speed:* **56.3 km/h**
*Danger Rating:* **3**

Each player chooses a dinosaur from these cards and take it in turns to agree a stat to compare – whoever has the biggest stat wins that round.

For example: a Triceratops might beat a Brachiosaurus with its danger rating, but the Brachiosaurus will outdo the Triceratops on weight!

### Maiasaura
*Size:* **4 metres**
*Length:* **9.1 metres**
*Weight:* **2.7 metric tons**
*Speed:* **24.1 km/h**
*Danger Rating:* **2**

### Parasaurolophus
*Size:* **5 metres**
*Length:* **12.2 metres**
*Weight:* **3.2 metric tons**
*Speed:* **32.2 km/h**
*Danger Rating:* **3**

### Iguanodon
*Size:* **6 metres**
*Length:* **10.1 metres**
*Weight:* **3.6 metric tons**
*Speed:* **40.2 km/h**
*Danger Rating:* **4**

### Microraptor
*Size:* **1 metre**
*Length:* **0.6 metres**
*Weight:* **0.9 kilograms**
*Speed:* **48.3 km/h**
*Danger Rating:* **3**

### Compsognathus
*Size:* **1 metre**
*Length:* **0.9 metres**
*Weight:* **2.3 kilograms**
*Speed:* **56.3 km/h**
*Danger Rating:* **4**

### Corythosaurus
*Size:* **5 metres**
*Length:* **9.1 metres**
*Weight:* **3.2 metric tons**
*Speed:* **24.1 km/h**
*Danger Rating:* **2**

### Argentinosaurus
*Size:* **10 metres**
*Length:* **30.5 metres**
*Weight:* **100 metric tons**
*Speed:* **8 km/h**
*Danger Rating:* **2**

### Carnotaurus
*Size:* **5 metres**
*Length:* **9.1 metres**
*Weight:* **3 metric tons**
*Speed:* **40.2 km/h**
*Danger Rating:* **9**

### Utahraptor
*Size:* **3 metres**
*Length:* **6.1 metres**
*Weight:* **0.9 metric tons**
*Speed:* **56.3 km/h**
*Danger Rating:* **8**

### Velociraptor
*Size:* **2 metres**
*Length:* **1.8 metres**
*Weight:* **68 kilograms**
*Speed:* **64.4 km/h**
*Danger Rating:* **9**

# TYRANNOSAURUS REX

A super famous apex predator from the Late Cretaceous!

 Natural History Museum

## Hunt and Scavenge

T. rex is one of the most famous dinosaurs of all time! It lived during the Late Cretaceous period in what is now North America. This mega hunter had many special adaptations that allowed it to seek out live prey, but it is thought it would also scavenge on dead animals.

## Tiny Arms

Like many other theropods, T. rex had small arms that would have been almost useless for hunting. One theory to explain this adaptation is that the dinosaur's incredibly powerful legs overtook the need for it to develop strong arms.

Long tail

Strong legs

## DINO FACTS

Name: *Tyrannosaurus rex (T. rex)*

Meaning: *"Tyrant Lizard King"*

Size comparison:

Food: *Meat*

Danger rating: *10/10*

Where: *Woodlands, floodplains, savannas*

## Pack Animal?

Fossils found at a few different sites in North America suggest that T. rex may have lived and hunted in groups, like wolves. This theory is still up for debate!

## Glossary box:

A **scavenger** is an animal that searches for and eats animals that have already died.

Large brain

Up to 6 metres tall

Banana-sized teeth

Small arms

## Deadly Bite

T. rex had huge jaws filled with razor sharp teeth and a bone-crushingly strong bite. It would have been able to eat huge amounts of meat in one go! When it lost teeth, new ones grew to replace them.

**MINI Activity**

## SHADOW MATCH

Only one of these shadows matches this picture of a T. rex, can you spot which one?

1    2    3    4

Answers on page 69.

# Dinosaur Detective

Now it's your turn to be a scientist! Can you research your favourite dinosaur?
Ask your grown up to help you search for all the information and record it below.

**NAME:** ................................................................

**HEIGHT:** ................................................................

**LENGTH:** ................................................................

**WEIGHT:** ................................................................

**DIET:** ................................................................

**WHERE IT LIVED:** ................................................

**WHEN IT LIVED:** ................................................

**DESCRIPTION:** ................................................

................................................................

................................................................

................................................................

**EXTRA FACTS:** ................................................

................................................................

................................................................

................................................................

Can you sketch a picture of your dinosaur here?
You could draw the whole dinosaur, its footprints, or its fossil!

# True or False Quiz

See how many of these quiz questions you can answer.
All the answers can be found in this annual.

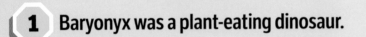

**1** Baryonyx was a plant-eating dinosaur. **True** **False**

**2** Carnotaurus had long, powerful arms. **True** **False**

**3** Gallimimus was a very fast runner, almost like a speedy bird. **True** **False**

**4** Oviraptor cared for its own eggs and babies. **True** **False**

**5** Apatosaurus means "thunder lizard." **True** **False**

**6** Diplodocus was one of the smallest dinosaurs ever found. **True** **False**

**7** Sinosauropteryx had feathers on its body. **True** **False**

**8** Therizinosaurus used its long claws to climb trees. **True** **False**

**9** Dimetrodon was an early ancestor of mammals. **True** **False**

**10** Triceratops had three facial horns. **True** **False**

**11** Mosasaurus was a dinosaur that lived on land. **True** **False**

**12** Tyrannosaurus rex means "tyrant lizard king." **True** **False**

*Circle the correct answer!*

*Answers on page 69.*

## p.16 DINOSAUR MEGA MAZE

## p.17 TRICKY WORDSEARCH

Mosasaurus is the only one that isn't a dinosaur

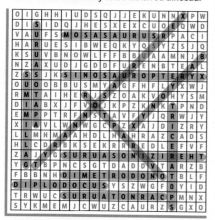

## p.21 FIND THE ODD ONE OUT

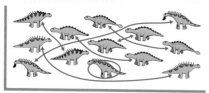

## p.25 BUILD THE PATH

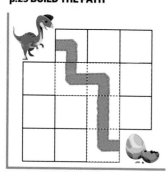

## p.31 FINDING FOOD

Line 3 leads the dinosaur to its dinner

## p.52-53 DINOSAUR HUNT

## p. 32 METEORIC MATHS!

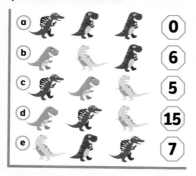

a. 0
b. 6
c. 5
d. 15
e. 7

## p.35 SHADOW MATCH

Shadow d matches the Diplodocus

## p. 41 HOW MANY WORDS?

Here are just some of the words that can be formed using the letters in Sinosauropteryx: Air, Art, Ear, Eat, Export, Iron, Noise, Nose, Paint, Pair, Party, Pass, Pear, Port, Poster, Press, Prey, Rain, Ray, Report, Reason, Rise, Roast, Rope, Rose, Rust, Snore, Sour, Spine, Spy, Star, Stay, Stone, Store, Story, Tax, Train, Treason, Trip.

## p.45 WHICH WAY?

Line 2 leads Therizinosaurus to the eggs

## p.47 PUZZLE MISSING PIECE

## p.50-51 SEARCH AND FIND

## p.56 DINO FOOTPRINT TANGLE

A. Spinosaurus
B. Ankylosaurus
C. T.rex
D. Stegosaurus

## p.65 SHADOW MATCH

Shadow 2 matches the picture of a T.rex

## p.68 TRUE OR FALSE QUIZ

1. Baryonyx: False
2. Carnotaurus: False
3. Gallimimus: True
4. Oviraptor: True
5. Apatosaurus: False
6. Diplodocus: False
7. Sinosauropteryx: True
8. Therizinosaurus: False
9. Dimetrodon: True
10. Triceratops: True
11. Mosasaurus: False
12. Tyrannosaurus rex: True